Whales fascinate us because of their huge size, their playfulness, their spouting, their intelligence, their "language" or way of communicating with one another, and their being warmblooded like us. We are also concerned because they have been hunted and harpooned until they are in danger of becoming extinct.

Richard Armour, writing of whales with his unique blend of fun and fact, finds them the freest of creatures, with no nest, hole, or cave. Since their home is the whole ocean, "they never leave home." In his playful verse, admired by the late Ogden Nash for its "wit and variety," and with everything carefully checked by experts, he tells of the ancestry of whales on land, the two main types ("toothed" and "toothless" or "whalebone"), such species as the Blue, Killer, Humpback, Right, Bottlenose, Pilot, Sperm, and others, and pictures their happy life with their friends.

For the eighth time, Paul Galdone has joined his delightful, action-filled drawings with Richard Armour's engaging verse.

SEA FULL OF WHALES

Dedicated to Michael Nichols,
a whale enthusiast, whose
spoutings on the subject
first brought it to my attention.

I am also grateful to Julius Schwartz,
Science Consultant, who never let me
stray far from the facts amidst
all the fancy and playfulness.

Other books for young readers
by Richard Armour
with pictures by Paul Galdone:

THE ADVENTURES OF EGBERT THE EASTER EGG
ALL SIZES AND SHAPES OF MONKEYS AND APES
ANIMALS ON THE CEILING
A DOZEN DINOSAURS
ODD OLD MAMMALS
WHO'S IN HOLES?
THE YEAR SANTA WENT MODERN

Also by Richard Armour
with a Foreword by Ogden Nash:

ON YOUR MARKS: A PACKAGE OF PUNCTUATION

And by Richard Armour
with drawings by Eric Gurney:

THE STRANGE DREAMS OF ROVER JONES

SEA FULL

RICHARD ARMOUR

123456789 RABP 7987654
Cataloging in Publication Data appears on last page.

OF WHALES

Paul Galdone
drew the pictures

McGRAW-HILL BOOK COMPANY

New York   St. Louis

San Francisco   Montreal   Toronto

W hat's that out at sea like a ship with no sail?
The chances are good
What you see is a whale.
And where there is one
There are two,
Maybe twenty,
For whales enjoy whales—
And of friends they have plenty.

They slide through the water
With greatest of ease,
And like sleek submarines
They descend when they please.
They rise to the surface,
They spout and they spray,
And then down they dive—
Up and down
All the day.

Oh, the life of a whale is a life that is free:
A whale finds it fun, I am sure, just to be.

The ocean is long
And the ocean is wide,
And there's room to the front,
To the rear,
To the side.
No trouble with traffic,
No stoplights of red,
A whale can keep swimming for hours straight ahead.
And when he grows tired
Does he seek out a nest,
A hole
Or a cave
Or a house,
There to rest?
No, wherever he is, he just stops there and naps,
Rocked to sleep by the roll of the ocean perhaps;
There he rests till he's rested
And ready to roam.
Since his home's the whole ocean,
He never leaves home.
A whale may swim
And a whale may swish,
But it isn't, it isn't, it *isn't* a fish.

A whale, like a dog,
Like a cat,
Like a camel,
Like a cow, like a horse, and like you
Is a mammal.

A fish is cold blooded,
A whale, though, is not.
Its blood stays as warm
In cold water as hot.
A fish takes in water, gets oxygen out of it;
A whale breathes in air and has lungs—there's no doubt of it.
A fish has a tail that it swings
Side to side
To send it ahead on a slithering ride.
But the tail of a whale ends with flukes flat as fans;
These it flaps up and down
And thus moves where it plans.

What makes it a mammal the most is the fact
That it nurses its young—
A most *un*fishlike act.
Yes, she feeds it with milk, which with motherly pride
She squirts from the nipples she has in her side.

So don't say a whale is a fish—no, not once,
Or a whale, if it heard,
Would say, "Oh, what a dunce!"

Whales' ancestors, land beasts,
Had arms, legs, and hair,
Then moved to the ocean,
Preferring it there.
The water supported their bodies just right,
And those that were heavy felt pleasantly light.
Their shape became streamlined,
Some sported a fin;
Their hands became flippers,
Most hair left their skin.
Today they just swim—needn't walk, sit, or stand,
And wonder why *anyone* lives on dry land!

What first, may I ask, comes to mind when you think
About whales? Well, I'll tell you as quick as a wink.
You think of their size,
As you often inform us:
They're big as a building,
They're huge,
They're enormous.

You're right, for the whale is the largest by far
Of creatures that were
Or of creatures that are.
The biggest of whales, the one known as the Blue,
Is bigger than elephants,
Dinosaurs too.

A Blue, when it's born, is as big as a bus,
It's twenty feet long,
Or it's twenty feet plus,
While a hundred feet long it can be, a grown male,
And that, I would say, is a whale of a whale.
And as for its weight—well, the largest, they say,
Might weigh what two thousand grown people would weigh!

There are two types of whales,
One the "toothed,"
One the "toothless,"
And the toothed to the toothless can really be ruthless.
Or some call the kinds
"Toothed" and "whalebone" instead,
Thus avoiding the "toothless,"
Though both can be said.

Blue
(Sulphurbottom)

The Blue whale is one that, to tell you the truth,
Has a mouth that is huge and yet hasn't a tooth.
He eats thanks to whalebone,
Oft known as baleen,
That hangs from the top of his mouth like a screen.
And Blue lets in water,
Then lowers this curtain
That serves as a sort of a strainer, for certain.
Up against the baleen, Blue then places his tongue
And presses it hard, as he learned when quite young.
The water goes out,
But it cannot be followed
By shrimp and the like
That remain to be swallowed.
Says Blue to himself, having done with this doing:
"My dinner's so dainty, why bother with chewing?"

Though Blue is so big, he's as nice as you'll meet.
He hurts not a thing, save the shrimp he must eat.

He asks but to swim with his friends and relations,
Enjoying the ocean,
Not just on vacations.
Blue swims all the seas,
North and south,
East and west,
But because of the food
The Antarctic likes best.
He's huge, but he's gentle, you cannot deny:
As peaceful as you
And as peaceful as I.

Killer
(Grampus)

Alas, not the same, I regret, can be said
Of the whale that's called Killer
That kills others dead.
Much smaller than Blue is, sharp teeth fill his jaws,
And with murderous muscles
He chews and he chaws.
On his back, sticking up, is a fin six-feet high
Like the frightening flag that a pirate would fly.
With his friends, a fierce gang,
Killer circles his prey—
One after another they nibble away.
Blue flaps with his flukes,
Which he swings like a swatter.
He churns and he turns
And he stirs up the water.

But Killer keeps coming, along with the others,
His gangsterish friends and his cousins and brothers.
And if he can manage,
From north or from south,
He sticks his head,
All of it,
Into Blue's mouth
And bites off Blue's tongue,
Or a sizable hunk,
Without which poor Blue slowly sinks
And is sunk.

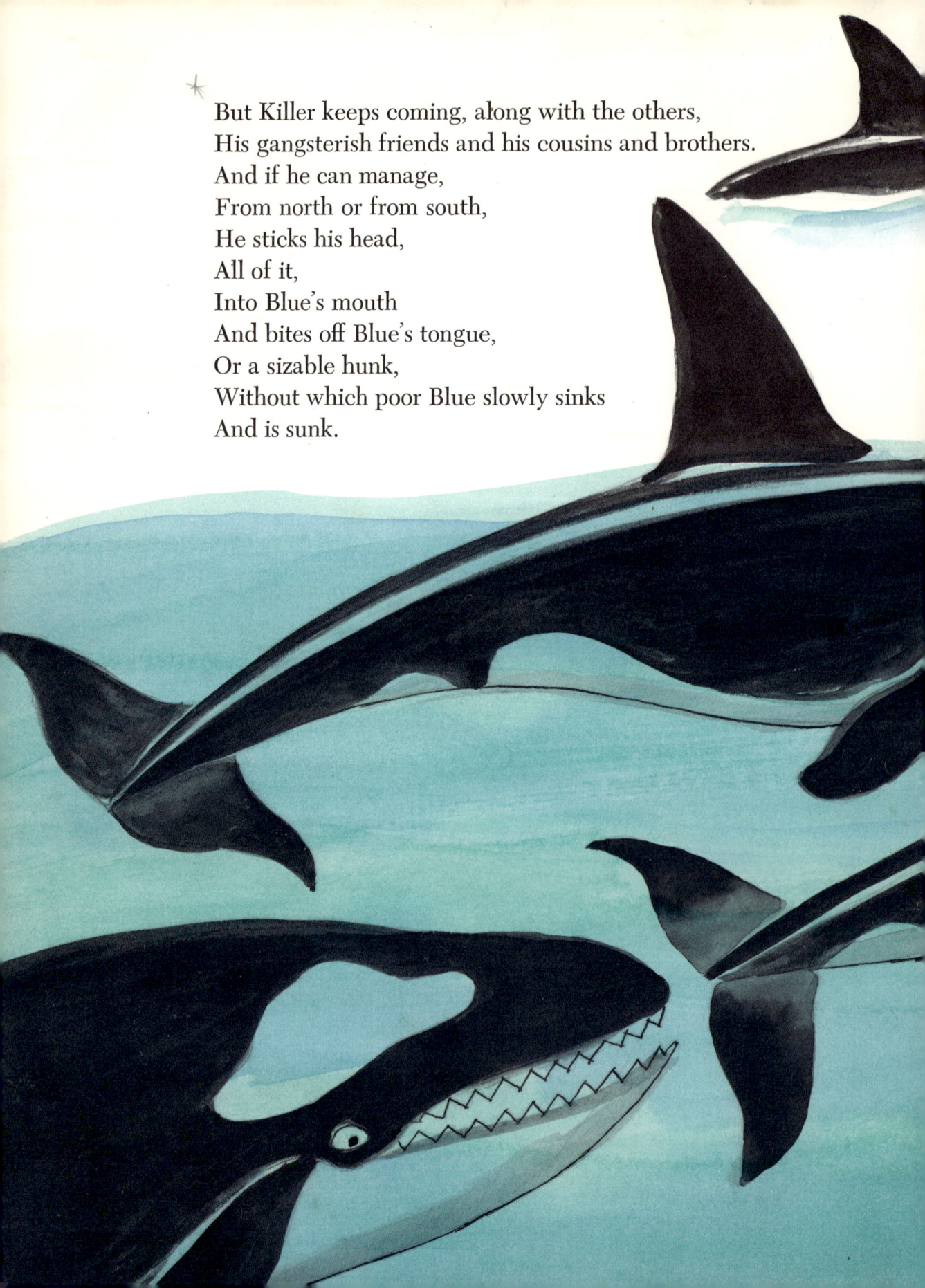

But bad as he is to such creatures as Blue,
He'd not do a thing to a human like you.
And so if a Killer you happen to meet,
Be glad there are others
He'd much rather eat.

Humpback

The Killer, they say, is the wolf of the sea,
But whales, as a whole, are more kindly than he.
Consider the Humpback, a bit of a clown,
Who swims under water,
Way down,
Way, way down,
Then suddenly leaps from the water, all dripping.
And maybe his flippers like wings he is flipping.
He even can stand on his head
Flapping flukes
And sending up spray
That's like watery spooks.
It's said near Bermuda
Along about June
At night he and friends
Sing a whale-music tune,
Yes, sing like a glee club or maybe a choir,
Though possibly not in the key you desire.
I'm sure that the Humpback,
Who plays without pause,
Would like to be noticed and win your applause.

Each summer, each winter, whales swim back and forth,
Finding water that suits them in south or in north.
Wouldn't *you* like to have such a huge swimming pool,
One end of it warm
And the other end cool?

They swim in a school or a gam or a herd
Or a "pod" if you'd use such an odd-sounding word.
And if you should use it,
Make plain, if you please,
It's a pod full of whales,
Not a pod full of peas!

Finback

A cousin of Humpback's,
Less playful and humorous,
Is Finback, the whale that was once the most numerous.
He has a flat head, much too flat for a hat,
But smiles a big smile (or he seems to), at that.
Toward the back of his back,
Like a slightly curved pin,
Is, as you'd expect of the Finback, a fin.
It isn't as large as the Killer's, oh no,
For it rises not more than ten inches or so.
But it helps Finback balance
While swimming full speed,
And Finback's full speed is quite speedy indeed.
He's graceful and slender,
He's built like a yacht—
Or like a torpedo—and off like a shot.

What helps you in spotting a whale out at sea
Is its geyser-like spout,
Spurting high as a tree.
It comes from the blowhole on top of its head
And fifty feet up, like a fountain, it's spread.
"Thar she blows!" you may cry
Just to prove that you know,
Like a sailor
Or whaler,
A spout is a blow.

Most think a spout's water,
But really it's not.
It's air the whale's held
In its lungs till it's hot,
And when the whale "blows" this stale air in a stream,
It condenses and looks like a teakettle's steam.
Haven't *you*, some cold morning, breathed warmish air out?
If you have, then you know what a spout's all about.

Right

Consider the whale known as Right, with a spout
You can tell from a distance and have not a doubt.
Unlike other spoutings
You ever will see,
His spout is divided
And looks like a V.
Now don't ask me why, for I really can't say.
Perhaps from a Killer he's just got away,
And he's happily blowing to show all is fine
And the V of that spout
Is a Victory sign.

The Right is called Right because whalers once sought him
And often, too often, harpooned him and caught him.
He was slow,
Had no teeth,
Had the oil they were seeking.
"He's the *right* whale," they said,
When of whales they were speaking.
The whalers were right about Right,
And so deft,
That not many Rights, sad to say,
Now are left.

Oh, birds have their feathers
And beasts have their fur,
So why, when it's icy,
Don't whales mutter, "Brrr?"
It's true some have hairs on their chin and their snout,
But so few you could count them—
They *don't* keep cold out.

The whale is, however, somewhat of a wonder:
Not over his skin, like a sweater, but under,
Yes, under what looks like a wet-suit of rubber
The whale has a layer of fat
Known as blubber.
The whales in the Arctic have blubber that's thicker
Than whales where it's warmer,
And what could be slicker?
Their babies, moreover, more tender and small,
Have blubber, like blankets,
That's thickest of all.

Bottlenose
(Beaked)

One whale I should mention,
A bit of a freak,
Is a whale that's called Bottlenose.
Boy, what a beak!
Whether friends call him Bottlenose, though, I would doubt,
At least not with Bottlenose swimming about.
He's lucky at that, for his friends might instead,
After looking again,
Call him Pointy Head,
Or possibly Four Teeth. (He never has more,
And I doubt he could buy a new set at the store.)

Narwhal

But Bottlenose probably thinks he looks good
Compared with the Narwhal
(As any whale would).
What makes him look odder than most whales you'll meet
Is a tooth that sticks out
Not an inch
But six feet!
Whatever you call it, a tusk or a tooth,
He should have worn braces when young—
That's the truth.
And yet it is useful if not ornamental,
And Narwhal is glad for development dental.
When under the ice in the Arctic
(Not rare),
He sticks it up through,
Makes a hole to get air.
So you never can tell. Something hardly a beauty
May come in quite handy—
We shouldn't be snooty.

Do I think a whale talks?
Well, he whistles for help
And he warns friends of danger
With yip and with yelp.
He whines and he chirps and he mews and he smacks
And he barks and he snorts and he clicks and he clacks.
Since his eyes aren't much good
And the water around
May be murky, at that,
He depends upon sound.

So he not only talks (though I'd need a translation)
But uses his sonar to get his location.
He gives but a squeak
Or a groan or a grunt,
And the echo comes back—
And he knows what's in front.
It may be a ship or a fish. Can you beat it?
He knows where and what
And can dodge it
Or eat it.

Pilot
(Blackfish)

One whale surely knows
How to signal to others,
To those in his pod,
Whether cousins or brothers.
And that is the Pilot, as sleek as a cat

Except for a forehead that bulges
(With fat).
His mouth is curved upward
Each side of his chin,
And asleep or awake there's a Cheshire cat grin.
His reason for grinning I'm guessing might be
That he's learned in whale language to say,
"Follow me."

That's why he's called Pilot.
He pilots his pod
And they go where he tells them
By sound or by nod.
Why they follow his lead, there is no way of knowing.
"I hope," they must say,
"That he knows where he's going."

Dolphin and *Porpoise*

But whales aren't all large,
There are small ones as well,
And of two I should like very briefly to tell.
These are Dolphins and Porpoises,
Both of them whales
Or "cetaceans" at least, if your argument fails.
The Porpoise is smaller,
Six feet at the most,
While the Dolphin a length
Twice as lengthy can boast.
The snout of a Porpoise is short
And quite blunt,
While a Dolphin has more of a beak up in front.
The Porpoise prefers to stay close to the shore;
The Dolphin is found far at sea much, much more.

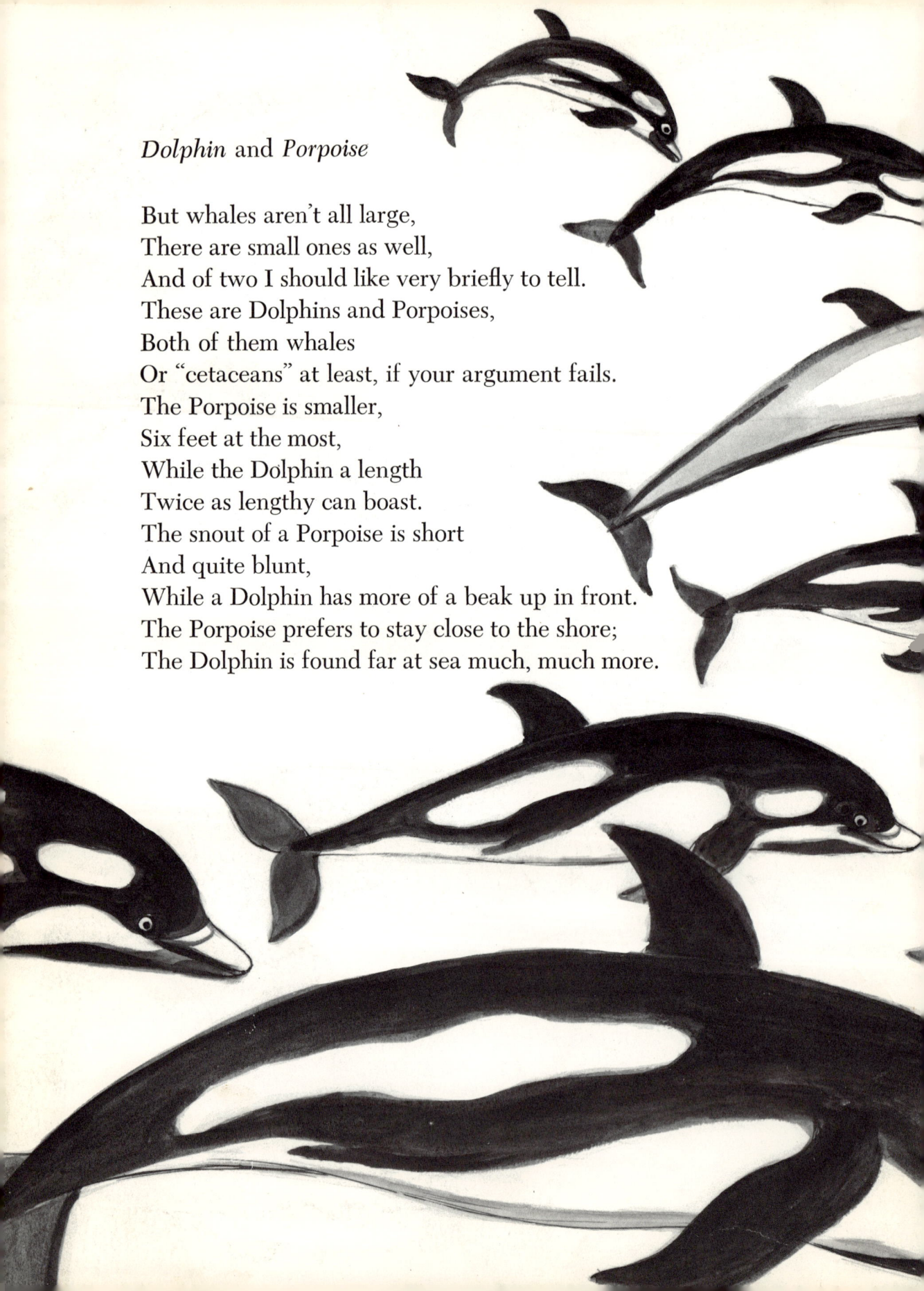

"See the porpoises playing,"
They'll bring you the news
If you're out on a ship,
Let us say on a cruise.
But really and truly it's dolphins, I'd bet,
Though it's not worth a quarrel or getting upset.
Both Dolphins and Porpoises,
Leaping and turning,
Are also intelligent,
Whizzes at learning.
Some say that for learning with quickness and ease
They rank right up next to those smart chimpanzees,
And maybe, just maybe
(I say, as a fan),
If second at all
They are second to Man.

Sperm

There are Gray whales and Sei whales and others galore,
But enough is enough.
I'll just mention one more.
The Sperm whale is next to the Blue whale in size,
With a head that is huge
But with wee, tiny eyes.
His snout is so square and so sawed-off a hunk
That it looks like a very large box or a trunk.
And his teeth, are they big?
They're like ivory mounds,
Each ten inches long
And weighing four pounds!
These teeth, although large and exceedingly tough,
Are all of them lowers—
But that is enough.
(He has but one blowhole,
While most whales have two,
But that, like those lowers,
Is enough,
It will do.)

His tail is so strong
And his dive is so deep
That a fighter of Sperm
Had best look ere he leap.
With his size and those teeth
That can hold
And can hack,

Sperm's the *one* whale the Killer
Will never attack.
And if he should try, I am sure he'd regret it.
To Killer I'd say, being helpful,
"Forget it."

Sperm's throat is so large that, if any whale can,
He could swallow (slurp, gurgle) an average man.
Only Sperm could have taken poor Jonah inside
And away on that really remarkable ride.

It was also a Sperm,
Moby Dick in this case,
That led Captain Ahab on such a wild chase
And shattered the *Pequod*
And, shattering hope,
Carried off the poor Captain,
All tangled in rope.

But Sperm has those teeth
And that throat
Not for men
But for squids with their suckers
And tentacles ten.
Down deep under water, Sperm squashes a squid
By ramming his head both abaft and amid,
Then nibbles its tentacles, gobbles the rest—
Though hard to believe,
Squid's the food
He likes best....

So there you've the whales,
As at home in the seas
As the beasts in the fields and the birds in the trees.
They play and they rest and they eat and they love
As they roam through the ocean
Below and above.
They've friends and they've families,
Just as have we,
And they swim and they spout
And they're glad to be free.
"It's great," they must murmur,
"Just being alive."
And they'll thank us, I think,
If we let them survive.

Library of Congress Cataloging in Publication Data

Armour, Richard, date
    Sea full of whales.

    SUMMARY: A rhymed introduction to the characteris-
tics of the various members of the whale family.
    1. Whales—Juvenile literature. 2. Dolphins—
Juvenile literature. 3. Porpoises—Juvenile literature.
[1. Whales. 2. Dolphins. 3. Porpoises]
I. Galdone, Paul, illus. II. Title.
QL737.C4A7   599'.5   73-13881
ISBN 0-07-002279-8
ISBN 0-07-002280-1 (lib. bdg.)

About The Author And Artist

RICHARD ARMOUR is an author who entertains readers of all ages. He has made a shambles of history (*It All Started with Columbus*, etc.), literature (*Twisted Tales from Shakespeare*, etc.), golf (*Golf Is a Four-Letter Word*), teenagers (*Through Darkest Adolescence*), education (*Going Around in Academic Circles* and *A Diabolical Dictionary of Education*), medicine (*It All Started with Hippocrates*), war and weaponry (*It All Started with Stones and Clubs*), and marriage (*My Life with Women*). He has also written such books of light verse as *Light Armour* and *Nights with Armour*. His latest books for children include *On Your Marks: A Package of Punctuation*, which has been made into a prize-winning educational film, *All Sizes and Shapes of Monkeys and Apes*, *A Dozen Dinosaurs*, *Who's in Holes?* and *The Strange Dreams of Rover Jones*.

A Harvard Ph.D. and author of scholarly books of biography and literary criticism, Richard Armour has had a long career of teaching at colleges and universities. In addition to being guest-in-residence on many campuses, he has lectured in both Europe and Asia as an American Specialist for the State Department. His writings have appeared in more than two hundred magazines in the United States and England, and this is his fiftieth book. He is married, has two children, and lives in Claremont, California.

PAUL GALDONE is one of the most successful artists in the children's book field. He has designed and illustrated a number of folktales, including *The Town Mouse and the Country Mouse*, *Old Dame Trot and Her Comical Cat*, and *Hereafterthis*. A country man, the artist divides his time between his home in Rockland County, New York, and his farm in Vermont.